Greedy Apostrophe

A Cautionary Tale

by JAN CARR

illustrated by ETHAN LONG

HOLIDAY HOUSE / New York

For Lois and Tess, good friends
who would *never* misuse an apostrophe
J. C.
For Carson, my little exclamation point!
Love, Dad

Greedy Apostrophe follows *The Chicago Manual of Style*, 15th edition (Chicago:
University of Chicago Press, 2003) and *Merriam-Webster's Collegiate
Dictionary*, 11th edition (Springfield, Mass.: Merriam-Webster, 2004).

Text copyright © 2007 by Jan Carr
Illustrations copyright © 2007 by Ethan Long
All Rights Reserved
Printed and Bound in Malaysia
The text typeface is Catseye Medium.
The artwork was created with ink pen on drawing paper,
then colorized on a computer.
www.holidayhouse.com
First Edition
1 3 5 7 9 10 8 6 4 2

Library of Congress Cataloging-in-Publication Data
Carr, Jan.
Greedy Apostrophe : a cautionary tale / by Jan Carr ;
illustrated by Ethan Long. — 1st ed.
p. cm.
Summary: Greedy Apostrophe runs all over town inserting himself
in places where he does not belong and causing great confusion.
ISBN-13: 978-0-8234-2006-3 (hardcover)
ISBN-10: 0-8234-2006-X (hardcover)
[1. Apostrophe—Fiction. 2. English language—Punctuation—Fiction.]
I. Long, Ethan, ill. II. Title.
PZ7.C22947Gre 2007
[E]—dc22
2006012114

The morning was hushed as the punctuation marks stumbled, still sleepy, still clutching their cups of cocoa, into Hiring Hall. A question mark hung over the hall. The question that all of the punctuation marks were asking was:

What jobs would they be assigned?

"Will they be good ones?" wondered the question marks.
"Of course they will!" exclaimed the exclamation points.

Their cousins the commas clustered excitedly. They too were eager to receive their assignments, for commas are a helpful bunch, as are punctuation marks in general.

Suddenly the quiet rustle in the hall was punctuated by the loud bang of the door. There stood a lone mark, a little curl—a little *sneer*—of an apostrophe, a mark known by all as

GREEDY APOSTROPHE.

"Shhh!" urged the exclamation points. "The meeting is about to begin!" The Director of Punctuation took his place at the podium. All the marks snapped to attention. It was time to recite the Punctuation Oath.

"On my honor I promise
To work with words, phrases, and sentences
To make their meanings clear.
I promise to uphold the rules of punctuation
And always to help readers, never to confuse them."

One punctuation mark, and one alone, refused to join in the oath.

That was

GREEDY APOSTROPHE.

"Rules schmules," he taunted.
"You've got it all wrong. It's more
fun to confuse readers—not help them!"

The Director took out his list of jobs
and began to dole them out.

"I have a DANGER sign in a construction
site," he said. "It needs an exclamation
point. Then over at the newspaper they
need quotation marks for the interviews
they're doing."

One by one the punctuation marks
stepped forward to fill their jobs.

At last the Director came to the jobs for the apostrophes. "I have some contractions," he said.

A cheer went up. Contractions were a favorite among the apostrophes, who were always happy to step in and serve as placeholders.

"There's a DON'T WALK sign over on Fifth and Elm. And three jobs in a song: 'Baby, I'm Here, You're Here, So Let's Dance.'"

Soon only one apostrophe was left.
One apostrophe and one job.
"It's for a possessive," said the Director.

At that all the other punctuation marks froze. A possessive? For Greedy Apostrophe? Oh no! He was always getting into trouble with possession!

"Greedy Apostrophe," said the Director. "Let me remind you. You are allowed to insert yourself before an *s* if that *s* is there to indicate that someone possesses something. For instance, in the phrase *Suzy's sweaters* or *Bob's bike*. When readers see you, they understand that something *belongs* to someone. Do you understand?"

Suzy's sweaters

Bob's bike

"Yeah, yeah," Greedy Apostrophe muttered impatiently.

"Also," said the Director, "there will be times when you must latch on to a plural to make the plural into a possessive. For instance, in the phrase *The Hoffmans' house*. In that case you are there to show that the house belongs to the family of Hoffmans. It's *your* job to make possessives—*not* plurals."

The Hoffmans' house

"Oh yeah?" jeered Greedy Apostrophe. "So how about *a*'s? Or *x*'s? Those're plurals, aren't they?"

The Director stood firm.
"Small letters and some
abbreviations are exceptions."
He glanced at his list.
"This job is for a sign
at a store," he said.
"TIMOTHY'S TOYS."

Greedy Apostrophe snatched the assignment and took off running. "Mine!" he cried maniacally. "All mine!"

As you can see, Greedy Apostrophe did have a great deal of trouble with possession.

"Remember," the Director shouted after him, "your job is to show possession. You are not there to make plurals. Period. End of sentence."

At the store, Greedy Apostrophe took his place in the sign. There he spied other signs, ones that also had *s*'s. Signs that read PUPPETS, MARBLES, yo-yos, and KITES.

PUPPETS

MARBLES

yo-yos

KITES

Quickly Greedy Apostrophe visited each and left his mark. The signs now read PUPPET'S, MARBLE'S, yo-yo's, and KITE'S.

The customers blinked, confused. What did the signs mean? Did they mean that something *belonged* to the toys?

After that Greedy Apostrophe disappeared into a magic shop. There he found more signs: CRYSTAL BALLS, WANDS, POTIONS, and CAPES.

These soon became CRYSTAL BALL'S, WAND'S, POTION'S, and CAPE'S.
More customers became confused.

Pencils

Erasers

Rulers

Books

Giddy with power, Greedy Apostrophe stole across the street to a school. There he slipped unnoticed into a classroom where someone—how thoughtful!—had posted more signs: PENCILS, ERASERS, RULERS, and BOOKS.

These he altered to read PENCIL'S, ERASER'S, RULER'S, and BOOK'S.

One alert student, Chloe Clarke, glanced up.

"Hey!" she cried, horrified. "Those apostrophes don't belong there!"

The children in the class acted quickly, for of course they all knew that apostrophes are not used to make words into plurals! They surrounded Greedy Apostrophe and chased him.

Unfortunately, they did not catch him. To this day, Greedy Apostrophe remains at large. Because of his behavior, Greedy Apostrophe is now banned from working as a punctuation mark. But that does not stop him. You will still come across him in places where he doesn't belong.

MELS' BANK

SPRITS' SODA

PACOS' TACO'S

HOT DOG'S

And so, dear reader, you must be watchful. You must take him away from any plurals that are not rightfully his.

Once and for all, Greedy Apostrophe must be removed . . .

"No!"

to the dreaded Punctuation Pen . . .

Math Problem's

$2 \times 2 = 4$ $5 \ = 25$

$3 \times 4 = $ 64

Apostrophe "S"

Claire's Computer
Mary's muffin
John's jumpsuit
greed ≠ good

"Anyplace but the pen!"
where the Director and Chloe Clarke
stand ready to teach him a lesson.

When Do You Use an Apostrophe?

Contractions

When a word or words are missing one or more letters, insert an apostrophe where the letter or letters are missing, for instance, can't, we've, let's.

Possessives

If a word is singular, you make it possessive by adding an apostrophe and an *s*, for instance, Suzy's sweaters. This is true even if the word itself ends in *s*, for instance, Charles's song. (Exception: some names from ancient times do not require an extra *s*, for instance, Moses' law.)

If a word is plural and the plural is formed by adding an *s*, you make it possessive by adding an apostrophe after the *s*, for example, the kids' bicycles.

If a word is plural but the plural is not formed by adding an *s*, you make it possessive by adding an apostrophe and an *s*, for instance, the children's toys.

Plurals

Apostrophes are used to make plurals with small letters and some abbreviations, for instance, b's and PhD's.

It's or Its?

It's (with an apostrophe) is a contraction. It stands for "it is." For example, "*It's* a dog." ("It is a dog.") Its (without an apostrophe) is possessive. "*Its* tail is wagging." Pronouns that are possessive—for instance, its, yours, and hers—do *not* use apostrophes.